Still to Mow

ALSO BY MAXINE KUMIN

Poetry

Jack and Other New Poems
Bringing Together: Uncollected Early Poems 1958–1988
The Long Marriage
Selected Poems 1960–1990
Connecting the Dots
Looking for Luck
Nurture
The Long Approach
Our Ground Time Here Will Be Brief
The Retrieval System
House, Bridge, Fountain, Gate
Up Country
The Nightmare Factory
The Privilege
Halfway

Novels

Quit Monks or Die!
The Designated Heir
The Abduction
The Passions of Uxport
Through Dooms of Love

Still to Mow

POEMS

MAXINE KUMIN

W. W. NORTON & COMPANY

New York   London

For information about permission to reproduce
selections from this book, write to Permissions,
W. W. Norton & Company, Inc.
500 Fifth Avenue, New York, NY 10110

For information about special discounts for bulk purchases,
please contact W. W. Norton Special Sales at
specialsales@wwnorton.com or 800-233-4830.

Manufacturing by Courier Westford
Book design by JAM Design
Production manager: Anna Oler

Library of Congress Cataloging-in-Publication Data

Kumin, Maxine, date.
Still to mow : poems / Maxine Kumin.
p. cm.
ISBN 978-0-393-06549-7 (hardcover)
I. Title.
PS3521.U638S75 2007
811 '.54—dc22

2007014704

W. W. Norton & Company, Inc.
500 Fifth Avenue, New York, N.Y. 10110
www.wwnorton.com

W. W. Norton & Company Ltd.
Castle House, 75/76 Wells Street, W1T 3QT

1 2 3 4 5 6 7 8 9 0

To Debbie

When you look back there's lots of bales in the field,

but ahead it's all still to mow.

— JOHN GARDNER

Contents

III | TURN IT AND TURN IT

IV | LOOKING BACK

I

Landscapes

Mulching

Me in my bugproof netted headpiece kneeling
to spread sodden newspapers between broccolis,
corn sprouts, cabbages and four kinds of beans,

prostrate before old suicide bombings, starvation,
AIDS, earthquakes, the unforeseen tsunami,
front-page photographs of lines of people

with everything they own heaped on their heads,
the rich assortment of birds trilling on all
sides of my forest garden, the exhortations

of commencement speakers at local colleges,
the first torture revelations under my palms
and I a helpess citizen of a country

I used to love, who as a child wept when
the brisk police band bugled *Hats off! The flag
is passing by,* now that every wanton deed

in this stack of newsprint is heartbreak,
my blackened fingers can only root in dirt,
turning up industrious earthworms, bits

of unreclaimed eggshell, wanting to ask
the earth to take my unquiet spirit,
bury it deep, make compost of it.

The Domestic Arrangement

from Dorothy Wordsworth's Journals

Wm went into the wood to alter his poems
writes Dorothy. *I shelled peas, gathered beans,*
and worked in the garden. This is Grasmere

where she picked and boiled gooseberries,
two lbs. of sugar in the first panfull
while *Wm went into the wood to alter his poems*

a trip he makes almost daily, composing
the lines she will later copy. Mornings
she works in the garden at Grasmere

which looked so beautiful my heart
almost melted away, she confides
while Wm's in the wood altering his poems.

On one of their daily walks she observes
helpful details of Wm's famed daffodils.
Then it's back to the garden at Grasmere

where she ties up her scarlet runner beans
and pulls a bag of peas for Miss Simpson.
Leave Wm in the wood to alter his poems;
praise Dorothy in the garden at Grasmere.

Today

Apples are dropping
all over Joppa
a windfall, a bagful
for horses and cattle.
Geese overhead
are baying like beagles.
The pears in the uphill
pasture lie yellow
a litter gone fallow
for stick pins of ground wasps.

The deer are in rut.
They race through the swales
and here on the marshy
spillway, a yearling
caught drinking, spies slantwise
two humans—us, frozen
unbreathing, the same pair
who tracked him slobbering
apples today in
our Joppa back pasture.

The Final Poem

Bread Loaf, late August, the chemistry
of a New England fall already
inviting the swamp maples to flare.

Magisterial in the white wicker rocker
Robert Frost at rest after giving
a savage reading

holding nothing back, his rage
at dying, *not yet,* as he barged
his chair forth, then back, *don't sit*

*there mumbling in the shadows, call
yourselves poets?* All
but a handful scattered. Fate

rearranged us happy few at his feet.
He rocked us until midnight. I took
away these close-lipped dicta. *Look*

*up from the page. Pause between poems.
Say something about the next one.
Otherwise the audience*

*will coast, they can't take in
half of what you're giving them.*
Reaching for the knob of his cane

he rose, and flung this exit line:
Make every poem your final poem.

Hunting Season

Target practice in the gravel pit
escalates once the date is set
to orange vests and whiffs of deer
immoderately helped by beer.

Yarded by stream, snagged in brush
Coors and Miller, bronzed and crushed
glint through fallen leaves and snow
to say no matter where we go

on trails that plunge vertiginous
their litter has preceded us.

Solstice

Blue jays back out of the forest
reduced to December beggary
hammering sunflower seeds
under the gash of tin roof,
frost staining the windowpanes
sour rime coating the pastures—
unpardonable to pass out and
wake with Winter, this stranger
in this cold home in this cold bed.

Xochi's Tale

Is it my fault I'm part rat terrier, part
the kind of dog who lives in a lady's lap?
I didn't ask to be bottom mutt in the pack
that runs untamed through the twisted trash-strewn streets
in Xochiapulcho, I didn't ask to be plucked
up by a pair of gringos. First, they took
away my manhood. No more sweet reek
of bitches, no hot pursuits, no garbage rot.
When they packed up to go back to the USA
I thought they'd cry, then dump me out, but no.

Macho mestizo, my entry papers say.
Who dines in style and sleeps the sleep of kings
ought dream no more of his rowdy half-starved days. . . .
I dwell in heaven but without the wings.

Virgil

He came, a dog auspiciously named Virgil,
homeless, of unknown breed but clearly hound
barking at scents, aroused by hot ones to bugle.
His first week here he brought three squirrels to ground
and lined their mangled corpses up on the grass
to be—why not?—admired before burial.
He gobbled the snottiest tissues from the trash.
Also, he swiped our lunches off the table.
He knew not *sit* or *stay*, has still to take in
that chasing sheep and horses is forbidden.
When reprimanded, he grovels, penitent.
He longs for love with all his poet's soul.
    His eyebrows make him look intelligent.
    We save our choicest food scraps for his bowl.

Come, Aristotle

On April 4, moving the pea fence
to another row, we unearth forty
perfect parsnips that have spent
the coldest winter since the seventies
condemned like leeches, Aristotle says,
to suck up whatever sustenance
may flow to them wherever they are stuck.
Overlooked. Our good luck.

Aromatic poppets, pried
from the black gold of old soil,
dingier than cauliflower or pearls,
we eat them braised with a little brown sugar.
Pure, Aristotle. Come, philosopher.
Come to the table. Sit by my side.

Six Weeks After

two roistering dogs splayed me flat
on frozen turf shattering six ribs
consigning me to gray walls, bleak thoughts
I'm up and about, hitching from place to place

and I see the common coarse-grained stones
have not given up their good seats in the wall
though the deckle-edged daffodils came and went
while I motored my rented bed up and down

and I see the greening margin along the road
is shaggy and unshorn and the goldfinches
have exchanged their winter costumes
for strobic lozenges of yellow that brighten

the window feeder and an indigo
bunting has brought his electric blue
to my sphere so that each time the rose-
breasted grosbeak alights for a sunflower chip

I am stunned into wholeness, healed
by a wheel of primary colors.

Essay, Freshman Comp

A student of mine turned in a composition
about shooting pigeons in his uncle's barn.
He peppered them with beebees.

They just sat there in the rafters
spots of red appearing on their breasts.
Eventually they toppled. The ones

that were still flapping he stomped on.
He says that he was eight or nine, he claims
that kids that age don't know what death is.

He's since become a vegetarian,
a lifetime of expiation ahead of him
in southern Ohio where's it's raining

on newly thawed fields and there's a nitrate
alert from all the fertilizer
washing down into the ground water,

contaminating local wells. They say
drinking it is still okay for grownups
though not for kids too young

to know what death is.

Elegy

C.K. 1929–1999

2 parts sugar, 1 part vinegar
my mantra while I shred, then chop
a head of purple cabbage hued so deep
it stains my fingers and the countertop

magenta-blue. Every September
each in our own kitchen we performed
this deconstruction of a perfect globe
lopped from the well-worked earth, then rubbed

clean enough to bring indoors. We stripped
its outer layers to the shiny sphere,
chopped, salted, set aside, readied for
2 parts sugar, 1 part vinegar. . . .

More than fifty years ago
you unearthed this innovative scrip
for freezer cole slaw from the Women's Page,
in your home town, Dayton, Ohio.

It ages well, or rather does not age
—*2 parts sugar, 1 part vinegar*—
old friend from Vietnam sit-in days,
the rain-soaked marches to stamp out Jim Crow,

you endured a cough that ran all summer.
That final meal, our mingled corn, slim ears. . . .
How could we cut you loose so suddenly?
So much unharvested, so much we did not say.

Parting

Enter November, wearing his helmet.
He watches me put the potato bed
to sleep under a blanket of rotted manure.
When March, all braggadocio and sleet,

bursts in, I will fork the faded horse apples
into the icy turf. As they break into grainy fluffs
my tines will exhume a few leftover marbles
of Norlands we seeded together last spring.

I will not put potatoes again in this bed.
When April comes, shy as a filly,
I will set out slim tips of sweet onions
you used to braid once they fattened.

Today you are farther away than ever,
the distant taillight of a car rounding
the downhill curve. Late. Cold.
I go in and uncork the white wine.

The Zen of Mucking Out

I never liked this stubbled field so much
as now, Keats wrote John Reynolds
and in my upper pasture I feel the same

where the last two horses of our lives
are at their day-long work reducing
the lightly frosted grass of mid-October

to manure, and I at mine, my five-
foot fork with ten metal tines, the hickory
handle worn down by my grip

so many years it almost seems to sweat—
muck basket to wheelbarrow, fork
upended till I reach the mother bed

and dump my smeary load, then stop.
White pine embroidery to the east,
a narrow view of Pumpkin Hill across,

lissome pond behind me. One late
garter snake sits sunning on an outcrop.
From the highway the vigor of sirens

announces a world of metal and speed
beyond my blinkered allegiance
to this task. My fingerprint,

my footstep. My zen.

II

Please
Pay
Attention

Please Pay Attention as the Ethics Have Changed

tag line, *New Yorker* cartoon, May 10, 2004

Four hundred and seventeen pen-raised pheasants
were rattled—think stick

on a picket fence—into flight
for the Vice President's gun. And after that

hundreds of pen-reared mallards
were whooshed

up to be killed
by, among others, a Supreme Court Justice.

Statistics provided by HSUS—
the Humane Society of the United States.

The exact number of ducks, however, is wanting—
this is canned hunting

where you don't stay to pluck
the feathers, pull the innards out. Fuck

all of that. You don't do shit
except shoot.

But where is that other Humane Society, the one with rules
we used to read aloud in school

the one that takes away your license to collar
and leash a naked prisoner

the one that forbids you to sodomize
a detainee before the cold eyes

of your fellow MPs?
When the pixie soldier says cheese

for the camera who says *please pay attention?*
The ethics have changed.

Fuck the Geneva Convention.

Extraordinary Rendition

Only the oak and the beech hang onto their leaves
at the end, the oak leaves bruised the color of those
insurgent boys Iraqi policemen captured

purpling their eyes and cheekbones before
lining them up to testify to the Americans
that, no, no, they had not been beaten. . . .

The beech leaves dry to brown, a palette of cinnamon.
They curl undefended, they have no stake in the outcome.
Art redeems us from time, it has been written.

Meanwhile we've exported stress positions, shackles,
dog attacks, sleep deprivation, waterboarding.
To rend: *to tear (one's garments or hair)*

in anguish or rage. To render: *to give what is due
or owed.* The Pope's message
this Sunday is the spiritual value of suffering.

Extraordinary how the sun comes up
with its rendition of daybreak,
staining the sky with indifference.

The Mindhunter

I'm a profiler.
I do serial killers.
I calibrate the messages.
I measure threat assessment.
The Bathroom Hacker,
The Night Stalker,
The Coastline Rapist
are all in my Solved Cases file.

I was at Waco, I studied
the blowout at Oklahoma City.
I'm big on stakeouts,
time spent surveilling
is never wasted. Nobody
knew more about the Unabomber
than I did, but my true
specialty is hostages.

I did Iran I and II.
I worked Somalia,
Colombia, Afghanistan.
A good negotiator gets inside
the mind of captive and his capturer.
My phone rings night and day.
My laptop's always on.
My website's *threatzall.com*

I dont have time to golf or ski
but in a pond out back
I'm raising koi, Japanese carp
orange, white and black.
Koi grow to fill up any
space you give them. I squat
down at the edge and feed
them every week or so.

Winters, I chop holes in the ice
so they'll have oxygen.
They lie there nose to tail,
packed in like canned sardines.
Imported canned sardines.
But I don't call them pets.
With all the worldwide threats
I don't have time for pets.

On Reading *The Age of Innocence*
in a Troubled Time

I read this curious Victorian novel
in the suspended bliss of a mid-July night.
Moths storm the screen, longing to plaster
their frail dust against the single bulb
that lights my page. It's 1870,
Old New York. Under the orange tree
Newland Archer kisses his fiancée,
May Welland, for only the second time
in their prescribed courtship and presses down
too hard in his ardor. As Edith Wharton tells it,
the blood rose to her face and she
drew back as if he had startled her.

Reading in bed before sleep, the luxury
of entering another world as if from above. . . .
I set it against the realities
of the breakfast table's news. Today
the *New York Times* unravels
the story of Mukhtaran Bibi, a Pakistani
woman who was raped as retribution
for something her younger brother
was said to have done, while the tribesmen
danced for joy. Gang rape. The definition,
several attackers in rapid succession,
in no way conveys the fervor,
the male gutturals, the raw juice as
the treasured porcelain of her vagina
was shattered. Splintered again and again.
And after, to be jeered at.
The shame of it.

What could Wharton's good virgin say
to this illiterate, courageous survivor
who dared to press charges?
                                —As if in her day
there were no tender girls turned prostitutes,
no desperate immigrants, no used-up carthorses
beaten to the pavement, their corpses
ravaged by dogs in Old New York. Look away,
May Welland! Turn aside as best you can.
Even defended from life on the streets,
from all that was turbulent, ragged and rough,
even unacknowledged, May, history repeats.
You must have seen enough.

Entering Houses at Night

None of us spoke their language and
none of them spoke ours.
We went in breaking down doors.

They told us to force the whole scrum
—men women kids—into one room.
We went in punching kicking yelling out orders

in our language, not theirs.
The front of one little boy bloomed
wet as we went in breaking down doors.

Now it turns out that 80 percent
of the ones in that sweep were innocent
as we punched kicked yelled out orders.

The way that we spun in that sweltering stink
with handcuffs and blindfolds was rank.
We went in breaking down doors.

Was that the Pyrrhic moment when
we herded the sobbing women with guns
as punching kicking yelling out orders
we went in breaking down doors?

What You Do

when nobody's looking
in the black sites what you do
when nobody knows you
are in there what you do

when you're in the black sites
when you shackle them higher
in there what you do
when you kill by crucifixion

when you shackle them higher
are you still Christian
when you kill by crucifixion
when you ice the body

are you still Christian
when you wrap it in plastic
when you ice the body
when you swear it didn't happen

when you wrap it in plastic
when the dossier's been there
when you swear it didn't happen
for over a year now

when the dossier's been there
for the ghost prisoner
for over a year now
where nobody's looking

for the ghost prisoner
when nobody knows what
you do when you're in there
where nobody's looking.

The Beheadings

The guillotine at least was swift. After
the head pitched sideways into a basket
and was raised to a thirsty crowd that roared
approval of death from above, the sun turned
a garish yellow and froze on the horizon
raying out behind the jellied blood the way
it once stood still over Jericho at Joshua's command
and the day held its breath. . . .

After they sawed through Nicholas Berg's neck
with an inadequate knife while he screamed,
after the heads of Daniel Pearl
and Paul Johnson were detached
in midthought, in terror but
caught alive on a grainy video, what
did their stored oxygen enable them to mouth,
and Kim-Sun-il who danced his last lines
declaiming over and over on worldwide television
I dont want to die what rose from his lips?

It was always night behind the blindfold.
Like bats in midflight at dusk
scrolling their thready messages come
words we can never capture, the soul
perhaps flying out from whatever aperture?
—a pox on belief in the soul!—and yet
there's no denying we are witness to
something more than
involuntary twitching going on

the air filling with fleeing souls
as it did in 1790, and filling again today
this poem a paltry testimony
to the nameless next and next—
Turks, Bulgarians, Filipinos whose heads
—severed, it is said the head retains
several seconds of consciousness—
will roll, reroll as in *revolution*
a time of major crustal deformation
when folds and faults are formed

time enough, in several languages
to recite a prayer, compose a grocery list
as the day holds its breath.

Revenge

Bugs in velvet-lined boxes,
bugs pincered into brooches,
bugs arrayed on platters,
bizarre collages more daring
than needlework, a fashionable
pastime for the leisure class.

Was this a way Victorian
ladies sublimated their rage?
Denied the vote, denied
divorce except with proof
of incest, bigamy, abuse,
denied the right to property,
even lands they came with. . . .
why not create a glittering
beauty out of silverfish,
mount ornaments of roaches,
medallions of beetles?

What impulse drives
this anatomically correct
4 x 6-foot papier-mâché
faux bas relief of a Japanese
beetle made of beetles?
Each individual
oval-shaped, 3/8ths inch long,
one-quarter wide, six legs,

two feelers, 37,000 corpses
tweezered into place with glue,
their green metallic backs—think
armor in Iraq—dulled by
the killer liquid. Four layers
of shellac will easily—
a piece of cake, a slam dunk—
restore their lustre.

The way they hitchhiked here,
arriving in New Jersey in
boxloads of freight from the Land
of the Rising Sun, the way
we let them spread, the way
we let them sucker us—
think *yellow cake, WMD*—
watching their emergence from
white grub to wings, we might as well
have handed them the Bill
of Rights to shred. Now they've chewed
their way northwest to Saskatoon.

I harvest them from leaves
reduced to lace, leaving the veins
behind, like used-up Rand McNallys,
flick them off to drown in
soapy water in the early cool

of the day. Sometimes they're locked
in postures of copulation, stacked
threes and fours, and fall
off easily, sometimes they're wary
and sweep away with a buzz.

It seems the more there are—
We are a nation that does not torture
—the more there are to catch and kill.
We weren't warned the levees might be topped.
There's pleasure in it, making art—
now we know that we're on amber alert—
of the garden's most voracious pest.

The Map of Need

On my laptop, terse as a police log,
the monthly list of where
the equine investigator's gone

    and in my lap, a catalog
    of child amputees, photos where
    the darling arm is gone,

        the perps mere boys who brag
        they're rebel soldiers now, Sierr-
        a Leonans, machete-clad for lack of guns.

How can it matter, then, a dozen
horses underweight? No water
no shelter, winter coming?

    Zambia. Dozens on dusty dozens
    in line for food and bottled water.
    When is the shipment coming?

        Through zoom lenses CNN pans
        babies at breasts empty of milk, whether
        the shipment will really come. . . .

December. Three horses barely able to stand
—even the hard-nosed sheriff concurs—
are trailered to hay, water, welcome.

Relief work's always moment to moment.
How wide is the map of need? Measure
the bellies enlarged on bark and roots, the maimed,

in the merciless heat and yet it soldiers on,
this rage, this will to live consumes, abides
wherever flesh is: everyone.

Waiting to Be Rescued

There are two kinds of looting,
the police chief explained.
When they break into convenience stores
for milk, juice, sanitary products,
we look the other way.

When they hijack liquor, guns,
ammunition, we have to go in
and get them even though
we've got no place to put them.

Hoard what you've got,
huddle in the shade by day,
pull anything that's loose
over you at night, and wait
to be plucked by helicopter,

saved by pleasure craft,
coast guard skiff,
air mattress, kiddie pool,
upside down cardboard box
that once held grapefruit juice

or toilet paper, and remember
what Neruda said: poetry
should be useful and usable
like metal and cereal.
Five days without shelter,
take whatever's useful.

Still We Take Joy

While in Baghdad sewage infiltrates
the drinking water and no one dares go out
to market, or goes, *inshallah*, praying
to return, and everyone agrees

it's civil war as it was in Virgil's time,
brother Roman against brother Roman,
warrior farmers far from their barren fields,
I am reading that *pastoral of hard work,*

as Ferry calls it, introducing his
translation of *The Georgics*, still a handbook
for gardeners two millennia later.
Last winter's sooty ashes are spread

and fields are fertilized with oxen dung
much as we do today, with cow and horse manure.
It's garlic we plant in autumn, beans, yes, in spring
in this fallen world that darkens and darkens.

On January 12th, an ice-locked day,
I dig three carrots, just as the poet instructs us
to take joy in the very life of things
so that, when Zeus comes down in spring

to the joyful bridal body of the earth
and the animals all agree it is time,
I can believe the wheel will turn
once more, taking me with it or not.

III

Turn It
and
Turn It

Revisionist History:
The British Uganda Program of 1903

A paradise in Africa?
How generous of the British
to offer a new Jerusalem
to the conference of Zionists,

an ample chunk of fertile land
to plow and plant, that the wandering
Jews might wander no more.

Dispatched, the three-man delegation
returned wild-eyed with tales
of lions, leopards, elephants
roaming the yellow veldt at will.

Also a warrior tribe, the Masai,
handsome as statues, whose cattle, given
to them by God, are their Torah.

In the words of Theodor Herzl:
The natives are to be gently
persuaded to move to other lands.
So far, this is history.

> But what if the Masai,
> proud lion hunters, laid down
> their spears, became willing partners?

First a trickle, then a torrent.
They came with wheelbarrows, seeds and hoes.
The proud Masai helped gather cow patties,
watched as these Jewish blacksmiths and tailors

devoutly turned them under the soil,
watched as grasslands gave way to gardens
heavy with peas, cabbages, melon.

What if the Jews grew browner,
the Masai grew paler until
the plateau was all café au lait?

To fatten the cattle the Jews raised alfafa.
The Tribe of Masai ate eggplants and greens.
They blessed each other's Torahs. Amen.
The wandering Jews wandered no more.

The Saving Remnant

Turn it and turn it
the old rabbis said
for everything is in it
except for the goddess
hatching her world-egg
except for the planet
she births from her navel
my father is in it
lifting his wine cup
breaking the challah
Fridays at sundown
my father declaiming
and it was evening
and it was morning
of the seventh day and
God rested on the seventh
day from all the work that
He had made the war in
Europe not yet started
my three older brothers
still at the table
who will ship out to
Rommel's North Africa
the Hump over Burma
the calm Caribbean
meanwhile my mother's hair
has not yet silvered
she fills the soup bowls
she serves the roast beef

rare at the center
and God saw that it
was good for hadn't He
chosen us from among
all people to survive.

I turn it and turn it
the parents have vanished
taking my brothers
one after another
and it was evening
and it was morning
I speak my own asides
into time's mirror
objects in the mirror
are closer than they appear
the past is as fragrant
as line-dried linens
my father the patriarch
laying the law down
my mother the peacemaker
straddling the yellow line
subversive subservient
nods to the goddess
hatching her world-egg
nods to the planet
she lifts from her navel
meanwhile still dwelling
inside his mother

David recited
a poem a poem
God cut out and saved to
paste in His scrapbook
the one that excludes us
who carry and give birth
who wash up and cover
what could He call it
the saving remnant.

O Sacred Fridays

In 1650 in the year of our Lord the Bishop
of Ussher deduced that October twenty-third,
four thousand and four B.C. was the first day of creation.

I can still hear my father reciting
over his silver shabbos cup *and it was evening*
and it was morning of the seventh day
and God rested from all the work that He
had made. The sixth day, when God formed man

of the dust of the ground, fell on October 29th,
and if on Monday, November tenth, Adam and Eve
were forced out of Paradise, this gave
them less than two weeks in the garden
before Eve bit into that apple.

And the Ark, said the good bishop, touched down
on Mount Ararat on May fifth, twenty-three thousand
four hundred and eighty B.C., but since archaeologists
are still finding bits and shards that may yet
yield to carbon dating, everything His Eminence
proclaimed may be skewed.

O sacred Fridays of challah and roast beef
when *it was evening and it was morning of the seventh day*
why did we rationalists repeat the liturgy
of Genesis and flood that we disbelieved?
Why did we—why do we now—cling to the salve
of repetition? And where is the bishop who will establish
the end-day of the world in the year of our Lord?

The day when the final creature will have sucked
the last lichen from the rocks, the day when the last
Inuit village above the Arctic Circle will collapse
in a cycle of starved polar bears, drowned baby seals?
That day when the village ghosts will come up
through breathing holes in the ice and the last
souls feed on souls.

The Immutable Laws

Never buy land on a slope, my father declared
the week before his heart gave out.
We bit down hard on a derelict dairy farm
of tilting fields, hills, humps and granite outcrops.

Never bet what you can't afford to lose,
he lectured. I bet my soul on a tortured horse
who never learned to love, but came to trust me.

Spend your money close to where you earn it,
he dictated. Nothing made him crosser
than wives who drove to New York to go shopping
when Philly stores had everything they needed.

This, the grab bag of immutable laws
circa 1940 when I was the last
child left at home to be admonished:

Only borrow what you know you can repay.
Your mother used to run up dress-shop bills
the size of the fifth Liberty Loan,
his private hyperbole. It took me years

to understand there'd been five loans
launched to finance the First World War,
the one he fought in, *the war to end all wars.*

What would this man who owed no man, who kept
his dollars folded in a rubber band,
have thought of credit cards, banking on line?
Wars later, clear as water, I hear him say

reconcile your checkbook monthly, and oh!
always carry a clean handkerchief.

Though He Tarry

*I believe with perfect faith in
the coming of the Messiah
and though he tarry I will
wait daily for his coming*
said Maimonides in 1190
or so and 44 percent
of people polled in the USA
in 2007 are also waiting
for him to show up in person—
though of course he won't <u>be</u> a person.

Do we want to save our planet,
the only one we know of,
so the faithful 44 percent
can be in a state of high alert
in case he arrives in person
though of course he won't <u>be</u> a person?

According to Stephen Jay Gould
 *science and religion are
 non-overlapping magisteria.*
 See each elbowing the other
 to shove over on the bed
 they're condemned to share?
 See how they despise, shrink back
 from accidental touching?
It's no surprise that
60 percent of scientists
say they are nonbelievers.

But whether you're churchy or not
what about the planet?
Damn all of you with dumpsters.
Damn all who do not compost.
Damn all who tie their dogs out
on bare ground, without water.
Damn all who debeak chickens
and all who eat them, damn
CEOs with bonuses,
corporate jets, trophy wives.

Damn venal human nature
lurching our way to a sorry
and probably fiery finale. . . .
If only he'd strap his angel wings on
in the ether and get his licensed
and guaranteed ass down here—
though of course he won't <u>be</u> a person—
if only he wouldn't tarry.

When the Messiah Comes

The first green pushing past the last snow,
the old horses in their spattered coats of rubbed plush
lined up facing downhill, sunbathing,
shedding great handfuls of hair toward the reckoning
when the Messiah comes up the sluicy drive
and the crows, holding nothing back,
halloo their praise.

IV

Looking
Back

Ascending

The grapes just forming are green beads
as tight on the stalk as if hammered into place,
the swelling unripe juveniles are almost
burgundy, promising yet withholding
and the ones they have come for, the highest
blue-black clusters wearing a dusting of white,
veiled dancers, tantalize in the wind.
Wrens weaving in and out, small bugs, pale sun.
Two bony old people in the back forty,
one holding the ladder, one ascending.

Looking Back in My Eighty-first Year

How did we get to be old ladies—
my grandmother's job—when we
were the long-legged girls?

—Hilma Wolitzer

Instead of marrying the day after graduation,
in spite of freezing on my father's arm as
here comes the bride struck up,
saying, I'm not sure I want to do this,

I should have taken that fellowship
to the University of Grenoble to examine
the original manuscript
of Stendhal's unfinished *Lucien Leuwen*,

I, who had never been west of the Mississippi,
should have crossed the ocean
in third class on the Cunard White Star,
the war just over, the Second World War

when Kilroy was here, that innocent graffito,
two eyes and a nose draped over
a fence line. How could I go?
Passion had locked us together.

Sixty years my lover,
he says he would have waited.
He says he would have sat
where the steamship docked

till the last of the pursers
decamped, and I rushed back
littering the runway with carbon paper. . . .
Why didn't I go? It was fated.

Marriage dizzied us. Hand over hand,
flesh against flesh for the final haul,
we tugged our lifeline through limestone and sand,
lover and long-leggèd girl.

The Outside Agitator

That winter of '42, a Radcliffe freshman,
I racketed to the end of the subway line
with three other classmates at 6 A.M.
where a well-bruised Union truck carried us off
to crouch at the Fore River Shipyard gates,
smitten with zeal to organize for the cause.

Two on each side, shivering, we leafletted
workers coming off the graveyard shift
swinging lunch buckets, lighting up their coughs,
and the day ones going in, swigging coffee dregs.
We got our asses pinched and phlegmy curses spat.
Some whispered *atta girl*. Most called us *dirty Reds*.

For twenty minutes we chanted *CIO*
as clots of women with grease-streaked faces
who earned one-third less than men for lob-
bing red-hot rivets eight hours on the job
punched out and drifted slowly past us,
part of the seventeen-thousand wartime force.

After the massive gates swung shut, the boss—
Irish, profane, longtime Union vet—
bought us breakfast at a railway diner
where we scarfed down bacon, biscuits
and a tower of pancakes swimming in Karo syrup,
a middle-class adolescent's finest hour.

And then an agent from the FBI
visited my father, 500 miles south:
your daughter is consorting with
known Communists. My father's voice
arrowed long-distance, unstoppable:
quit or leave school. End of call.

My father's daughter, I rose to the threat.
I'd get a live-in job, a scholarship,
picket for working women, write the script
for Ralph the Foreman, paunchy villain,
star of the Union paper's comic strip,
at rallies sing *There once was a union maid,*

I dreamed I saw Joe Hill last night,
and *Debout! les damnés de la terre!*
the first verse at least, of *The Internationale.*
Surrounded, I pushed back the dread
he'd planted, the vine called Communist
that spiraled secretly above my head.

What about this International Soviet?
A better world is in the birth, or was it?
Over Christmas I went hangdog home
to empty rooms, three brothers overseas
fighting in three different war zones.
Letters—called V-mails—came infrequently.

My mother's hair was falling out from worry.
Too many sons of family friends were gone.
Nightly, my father read the *New York Times*,
tuned in to Edward Murrow, H. V. Kaltenborn.
He never mentioned our fierce standoff again
but the memory of it adhered to me, like slime.

Once back in Radcliffe's arms, I shunned
my former Marxist friends, pleading a fever,
hour exams, term papers. Pressed, I swore
the FBI was out to get my father.
Guilt-slicked, half-believed, I signed off the list,
went back to reading Conrad, Joyce and Proust.

Old Friends

for Cleopatra Mathis

One moment you are stuck
and then the moment expands.
—Samrat Upadhyay

When long ago in Louisiana—
you were 20, he, 16—
outraged over his English grade
your student stuck

his pistol in your face, you said
I fainted standing up
but promptly came to
and demanded his gun which

you gave back to him
after class. He passed
the final exam, became
your devoted slave.

Forty years later, you roll
my wheelchair toward the stage,
my broken leg stuck out
in front of me like a sawed-off shotgun

and I rise in the lift to take
my place with the other
honorands. Rain threatens
then whooshes in.

Going down, the lift jams.
It's still pouring. While
I wait for Maintenance
to pry me out I play

this story in my head.
You've gone missing. See
how the moment expands?
They come with an umbrella

but you've run away with him,
a mathematics whiz; no,
a cocky state trooper
or the local dive's bartender

and here we are, old friends
evolving, aging, mending,
all three at once. We're
just getting started.

The Revisionist Dream

Well, she didn't kill herself that afternoon.
It was a mild day in October, we sat outside
over sandwiches. She said she had begun

to practice yoga, take piano lessons,
rewrite her drama rife with lust and pride
and so she didn't kill herself that afternoon,

hugged me, went home, cranked the garage doors open,
scuffed through the garish leaves, orange and red,
that brought on grief. She said she had begun

to translate Akhmatova, her handsome Russian
piano teacher rendering the word-for-word
so she didn't kill herself that afternoon.

She cooked for him, made quiche and coq au vin.
He stood the Czerny method on its head
while her fingers flew. She said she had begun

accelerandos, Julia Child, and some
expand-a-lung deep breaths to do in bed
so she didn't kill herself that afternoon.
We ate our sandwiches. The dream blew up at dawn.

During the Assassinations

I took the cello to its lesson,
the cheerleader to the gym.
I was a sixties soccer mom

and when the bassoon needed
double reeds to suck on
I scoured Boston.

I bought red knee-highs for the cheerleader.
Skirts wide enough to straddle
the cello onstage.

Cacophony of warm up, then
the oboe's A, *every
good boy does fine*, football

games with fake pompoms
siss-boom-ba and after,
gropings under the grandstands.

I went where I was called to go.
I clapped, I comforted.
I kept my eyes on Huntley and Brinkley.

During the assassinations
I marched with other soccer moms.
I carried lemons in case of tear gas.

I have a dream became my dream.
I stood all night
on the steps of the Pentagon.

With each new death
I added my grief
to the grief of millions

but always her pink suit
on the flat trunk of the limousine
and in her hand a piece of his skull.

The Lower Chesapeake Bay

Whatever happened to the cross-chest carry,
the head carry, the hair carry,

the tired-swimmer-put-your-hands-on-my-shoulders-
and-look-in-my-eyes retrieval, and what

became of the stride jump when you leap
from impossible heights and land with your head

above water so that you never lose sight
of your drowning person, or if he is close enough, where

is the lifesaver ring attached to a rope
you can hurl at your quarry, then haul

him to safety, or as a last resort
where is the dock onto which you tug

the unconscious soul, place him facedown,
clear his mouth, straddle his legs and press

with your hands on both sides of his rib cage
to the rhythm of *out goes the bad air in*

comes the good and pray he will breathe,
hallowed methods we practised over and over

the summer I turned eighteen to win
my Water Safety Instructor's badge

and where is the boy from Ephrata, PA
I made out with night after night in the lee

of the rotting boathouse at a small dank camp
on the lower Chesapeake Bay?

Cuba, My Brother, the Hangings

I

The morning the triple suicides
are trumpeted, I wake from a wild
dream of my brother the football star,
a sybarite with his mouth-wet cigars
and the pretty whores of his Florida-
Cuba weekend runs. It's old Havana
in the seamy days of Batista: bright sun,
bad blood, the screech of tires, no one
to blame, no one to know.
In the distance, Guantánamo.

Into the rich gambling gravy stirred
by Cuba's Capones imported from
New York, Las Vegas and Reno, comes
my brother the All-American guard.
In the Sans Souci he pulls the slots,
in the Nacionale he rolls the dice.
The deep crimson walls, the Turkish carpets
evoke the fifties, the rum-flushed lips
of my brother, his still-boyish face,
fingers stacking his winning chips.

II

The ghost of my brother observes when these three
loop their bedsheets over the top bar
and place their heads inside the slipknots
and jump from the lips of the toilets

—I am imagining this detail, as
the actual methodology has
not appeared in the *Times*—
their act at Gitmo becomes
manipulative self-injurious behavior,
an act of asymmetrical warfare.
In uniform now, my ghost-brother is there.

Appropriate psychological tests
administered shortly before
they made the necessary leap
confirmed they were not depressed.
They have insulted us, they have
spit on our flag, they deserve,
my revenant brother asserts, to dangle in
full view of the Geneva Convention
but now they will be
treated with cultural sensitivity.

An imam from Quantico will see
that the bodies—two Saudis, one Yemeni—
will be wrapped in white cloths and aligned
facing Mecca before they are reverently
airlifted to their native lands.
They need not be mentioned again.
My brother's pit bosses and dealers are gone
along with his monogrammed white-on-white shirts,
silk ties fastened with jewelled clips. His cock fights,
his prostitutes, his choice white rum remain.

As for the living who pace forever
in their spotless barren rage-proof cells
—unlike my brother with his comforts,
his women on call, his old Havana
of café con leche, graft-fissured highways—
they will age, they will die as caged beasts.
Meanwhile they are kept
in green antisuicide smocks
that cannot be torn into strips.
We will keep them alive whatever it takes.

Perspective

First learn perspective, Leonardo said
then draw from nature.

Stubbs's *Whistlejacket* answers
on a canvas nine feet tall

commissioned in 1762
by the Second Marquess of Rockingham.

This horse looks out
at any who look in, looks out

prickeared, exaggerated mane and tail
caught in a half-levade, hocks over heels.

O horse of my heart, hang on at this still point
as all around us open-air markets explode,

body parts rain down and families
rush to collect them, else no afterlife.

The priest insists that animals are sinless,
have no souls, won't appear in heaven,

his heaven, not the paradise
of expectant virgins. Where

Whistlejacket went is
not revealed, into the ground,

perhaps, in his final pasture,
O horse of my heart, full nine feet tall.

The Corset Shop

The heavy oak door of Madame Marguerite's corseterie
at a good address in downtown Philly

circa 1932, opens onto such pink
such rosy froufrou that the enchanted child thinks

she has wandered into a candy store.
Madame and her mother air-kiss three times while the armor

of their torsos cannot avoid making
contact with a small click. Her mother has come for a fitting.

Madame is so eager she glistens.
Business has slowed to a trickle. This is the Depression.

The child is shown to an armchair
that swallows her. She dozes in the perfumed air.

In the backroom a slavey bends over
a sewing machine stitching, reshaping, repairing. Her love

child, now three or four, plays on the floor with a doll.
This is all the incurious child can recall.

*

Each morning the child I am in this story watches transfixed
as her mother dresses in the shadow of her closet.

She works her way into the brittle frame that encloses
her body from waist-bulge to pubis

then bends forward, inviting her breasts, those floppy
   spaniels' ears
to slip into place in the brassière

that attaches with small hooks to the corset.
This is before I have breasts, or even a discernible waist.

My body is a smooth column
except for my shoulders; swimming has enhanced them

for I raced in the Y's events from the time I was nine
to my mother's despair. She does not attend.

And my long pigtails are always wet, smelling of chlorine,
ruining the family supper, or so she claims.

Pigtails that I am to hack off with a scissors
three years later. We wrangle over

them endlessly before each morning's redo:
Hold still! Your part is as crooked as Ridge Avenue.

*

I've just had my first period. I have come with my mother
to be fitted by Madame for a brassière.

There is nothing in stock broad enough to stretch
across my back, yet small enough to cup my just
    emerging breasts.

An item will have to be custom made. The two women giggle
over my barely engorged chest, my flat pink nipples.

Unforgivable, unforgettable, this scene.
I try to expunge it from my memory's screen

as the shop itself disappears,
the old neighborhood falls into disrepair

and Madame, nearly blind and by now quite deaf, totters
about the modest home of her daughter.

                    *

Now she is gone, let us remember my mother
in hat and gloves, in silk stockings, with appropriate
    purse no matter

the day's heat or cold, dressed as a lady dresses. Let us stop
on the disreputable daughter, braless behind some
    shapeless top

holding her mother's note.
I loved seeing you, it said in a tiny cramped script

that wandered downhill on the page. *Even though it was
so brief
I loved.* . . . The stroke that took her life

came on as gently as a Wedgwood pitcher might pour milk.
She died as she had often requested, in her sleep, uncorseted,
but in silk.

Death, Etc.

I have lived my whole life with death, said William Maxwell,
aetat ninety-one, and haven't we all. Amen to that.
It's all right to gutter out like a candle but the odds are better

for succumbing to a stroke or pancreatic cancer.
I'm not being gloomy, this bright September
when everything around me shines with being:

hummingbirds still raptured in the jewelweed,
puffballs humping up out of the forest duff
and the whole voluptuous garden still putting forth

bright yellow pole beans, deep-pleated purple cauliflowers,
to say nothing of regal white corn that feeds us
night after gluttonous night, with a slobber of butter.

Still, Maxwell's pronouncement speaks to my body's core,
this old body I trouble to keep up the way
I keep up my two old horses, wiping insect deterrent

on their ears, cleaning the corners of their eyes,
spraying their legs to defeat the gnats, currying burrs
out of their thickening coats. They go on grazing thoughtlessly

while winter is gathering in the wings. But it is not given
to us to travel blindly, all the pasture bars down,
to seek out the juiciest grasses, nor to predict

which of these two will predecease the other or to anticipate
the desperate whinnies for the missing that will ensue.
Which of us will go down first is also not given,

a subject that hangs unspoken between us
as with Jocasta, who begs Oedipus not to inquire further.
Meanwhile, it is pleasant to share opinions and mealtimes,

to swim together daily, I with my long slow back and forths,
he with his hundred freestyle strokes that wind him
    alarmingly.
A sinker, he would drown if he did not flail like this.

We have put behind us the State Department tour
of Egypt, Israel, Thailand, Japan that ended badly
as we leapt down the yellow chutes to safety after a
    botched takeoff.

We have been made at home in Belgium, Holland,
    and Switzerland,
narrow, xenophobic Switzerland of clean bathrooms and
    much butter.
We have travelled by Tube and Metro *in the realms of gold*

paid obeisance to the Winged Victory and the dreaded Tower,
but now it is time to settle as the earth itself settles
in season, exhaling, dozing a little before the fall rains come.

Every August when the family gathers, we pose
under the ancient willow for a series of snapshots,
the same willow, its lumpish trunk sheathed in winking
   aluminum

that so perplexed us forty years ago, before we understood
the voracity of porcupines. Now hollowed by age and
   marauders,
its aluminum girdle painted dull brown, it is still leafing

out at the top, still housing a tumult of goldfinches. We try to
   hold still
and smile, squinting into the brilliance, the middle-aged
   children,
the grown grandsons, the dogs of each era, always a pair

of grinning shelter dogs whose long lives are but as
   grasshoppers
compared to our own. We try to live gracefully
and at peace with our imagined deaths but in truth we go
   forward

stumbling, afraid of the dark,
of the cold, and of the great overwhelming
loneliness of being last.

Notes

The book's epigraph is taken from Terrence Des Pres's interview with John Gardner that appeared in the *Yale Review*, October 1983.

The quotation cited in "Come, Aristotle" is taken from George Santayana's *The Philosophy of Travel* as quoted in *Servants of the Map* by Andrea Barrett.

The material in "Entering Houses at Night" is taken from a young female Iraqi's blog dated February 11, 2006, written under the pseudonym Riverbend.

The material in "What You Do" is taken from "A Deadly Interrogation," by Jane Mayer, *The New Yorker*, November 14, 2005.

The quoted material in "Still We Take Joy" is taken from *The Georgics of Virgil*, translated by David Ferry, Farrar Straus and Giroux, New York, 2005.

A sidebar to "Revisionist History": in 1902, Joseph Chamberlain, British Colonial Secretary, offered five thousand square miles in the British Protectorate as a national homeland for the Jews in what was then designated Uganda. After fierce debate in 1903, the Zionist Congress agreed to send a group to inspect the land and in 1905 politely declined the offer.

The epigraph to "Old Friends" is taken from Samrat Upadhyay's story "What Will Happen to the Sharma Family," published in *Ploughshares*, Spring 2006.

All facts and quoted material in "Cuba, My Brother, the Hangings" are taken from BBC News, June 11, 2006, and an Associated Press dispatch dated June 28, 2006.

Acknowledgments

Some of these poems have appeared, sometimes in slightly different versions, in the following publications:

Alaska Quarterly Review
Alehouse Review
American Poetry Review
Atlantic Monthly
Bark
Caduceus
The Forward
Hudson Review
The Nation
New England Watershed
New Letters
The New Yorker
North Dakota Quarterly
OnEarth
Orion Magazine
Pleiades
Prairie Schooner
The Progressive
Shenandoah Review
Witness
The Women's Review

"The Final Poem" is reprinted in *Poems Inspired by the Life and Work of Robert Frost,* edited by Sheila Coghill & Thom Tammaro, University of Iowa Press, 2006.

"Entering Houses at Night" and "What You Do" are reprinted in *Caduceus, the Poets at Artplace,* edited by Anthony Fusco, Yale Medical Group, New Haven, 2007.

"Entering Houses at Night" is reprinted in *Pushcart Prize XXXI: Best of the Small Presses,* edited by Bill Henderson, Pushcart Press, 2007.

"Waiting to Be Rescued" is reprinted in *New Orleans and Other Poems,* Bayeux Arts, Calgary, 2006.